Raw and *Unspoken*

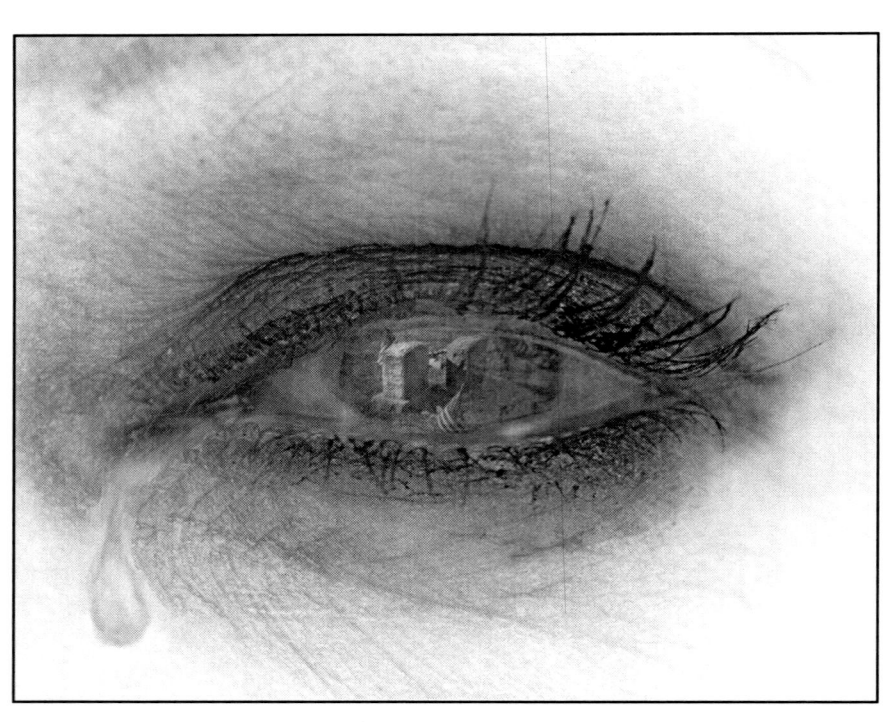

To a wonderful and loving mom, my heart is with you, Lesia

LESIA SCHOFER

Raw and *Unspoken*

A Memoir of Private Pain and Sorrow

iUniverse

RAW AND UNSPOKEN
A MEMOIR OF PRIVATE PAIN AND SORROW

iUniverse books may be ordered through booksellers or by contacting:

iUniverse
1663 Liberty Drive
Bloomington, IN 47403
www.iuniverse.com
1-800-Authors (1-800-288-4677)

ISBN: 978-1-4917-7055-9 (sc)
ISBN: 978-1-4917-7054-2 (e)

Library of Congress Control Number: 2015911403

Print information available on the last page.

iUniverse rev. date: 7/21/2015

In loving memory of my son, Christopher.

You left too soon, at twenty-five. You loved being a dad, and you loved people, cars, Chevys, motorcycles, beaches, and the sun.

You were happy, positive, and outgoing but also disciplined and hardworking.

You helped so many people in so many ways.

You will be sadly missed, always remembered, and forever loved.

Contents

Preface

At this time, this book is not about healing. I cannot discuss "moving on" or express that the pain of loss is becoming "softer." I'm sorry, but at this time, I can only openly express the shock, denial, and tearful agony of losing a child to death through a sudden tragedy. That is all that can be shared at this time. Perhaps some of you know what I mean. How many of us are the walking wounded, silently carrying a load unthinkable to some? Who out there also shares this feeling of agony? Does it feel as if you are the only one engulfed in this private pain and sorrow? For me, grief is similar to being shaken and uprooted by an earthquake and then being engulfed by the tides of a tsunami. I can't breathe; I can't see clearly at this time. It is difficult to speak when feeling raw to one's core. My hope is to share my journey of heartache as honestly as I can. If you share the pain or are comforted by any of the passages in this book, even for a little while, then we are not alone.

Acknowledgments

I am so appreciative of everyone who has been there to listen and help me during this time of sorrow and adjustment.

My angel son, because of you, I became a grateful, first-time mother. You and your brother are the blessings to my heart and soul.

Ed Martin, you are a great support and stable partner in life.

I thank my beloved son's immediate and extended family and friends for making his life full and rich and for continually loving him and treasuring his life and his memory.

Susan Broccolini-Laing, my beloved friend, who keeps our friendship renewed after so many years. Our sharing of honesty and emotions is priceless.

I am truly thankful to the helpful and caring organizations like TAPS (Tragedy Assistance Program for Survivors), Compassionate Friends Chapters, and SOS (Survivor Outreach Services) at Fort Dix.

A specific thank-you goes to Julianne Kennedy, my SOS support coordinator. Julie, you were there for me from the very beginning of this tumultuous journey. You are a wonderful listener and a constant support, with resources abundant.

I thank my grief counselor, Dorothy Lyons, MA, who believed in the value of my grief process and whose feedback was right for me then and today. I am eternally grateful for your helpful and needed guidance.

I thank Carmen Amalia Reveron, MSN, bereavement therapist from VA Readjustment Counseling Services, who provided such a supportive and understanding environment, with hope, during my grief recovery.

Introduction

I am a mother. As another Friday afternoon was nearing three o'clock, I was attempting to reach my son for a nice conversation. As minutes and then two hours passed, I became a bit unsettled because my call had gone unanswered. Little did I know that at four thirty, my son had been killed on his motorcycle in a collision with an automobile making a turn. At around a quarter after five, I received a phone call that made me feel like an atomic bomb had detonated within me.

I needed to express in words the pain and sorrow that had remained unspoken. I had churned these stirred feelings inward, but now I wished not to feel alone. I felt that others out there feel the same kind of pain. Sharing might help the world become a softer place. All that continues to be tangled and twisted together now rests in words expressed by shock, anger, love, and everything else. Grief has changed my life forever. Living without my child is a story of trying to survive at a crossroads between two worlds, one with him and one without him. What's left is the land of lost dreams and promises. Please follow me, hold me, support me, and listen to me—and I hope to do the same for someone else through my words.

No! Say It Ain't So!

Oh my God! Say it ain't so. From this second forward, do I bargain with fate? Please—let time go back just one second? Let this moment start over so that this did *not* happen.

Seriously, I did not hear or believe what I'd just heard. *I did not!* Over the telephone, I heard that my son was in a motorcycle accident and that he "passed" right then and there. It was the telephone call that changed many lives forever. I felt as if I were suffocating. I felt the air and life being sucked right out of me, instantaneously. It's as if I were a deer in headlights and a truck were ready to hit me head-on.

Time does stop; there is a silence that is indescribable, my mouth drops open, and my voice disappears. I have just been robbed! Frozen. Disbelief. Helplessness. Confusion. Sheer horror. Frozen. This sudden news is thunderous to me, but at the same time, it's unreal how shock has no sound. It's as if a silent bomb has gone off. Shrapnel is exploding everywhere, and all I can do is stand still and take it. I feel detached from my body parts. Shattered. Shock precedes the blunt-force trauma of emotional turmoil. Pieces of me will never be put back the same way again. There is a war zone in my core with no escape plan. I don't even realize I am hurt and injured. I now have a gaping hole in my heart, and I can't even weep because all of this

1

seems so unreal to me. I am naive and inexperienced about the hard work of impending pain and sorrow that I will carry for the rest of my life. I am frozen and none the wiser that when I thaw, it will hurt worse.

I bargain with my soul for another chance for my child to be okay. This is a cruel time warp, thoughts race in a loop, and I can't find my way out. It can't be real—I tell you; it just *can't*! Is that an elephant sitting on my chest that's making it so hard to breathe? Have you been in my shoes, and, if so, did you find it so hard to breathe? If I could just pass out, I wouldn't feel anything—I wouldn't remember anything. I don't like this "past tense"—that he died. No, take it back! My child is not to be spoken of in the past tense. Don't say he died. I will hate you if you say so. How cruel am I to think that "will die" or "dying" is more of a gift than "died." If he died, then I can't *get him back*. I want him back! Who the hell took him, and where did he go?

I am his parent. It doesn't matter how old my child is; he *belongs* to me. I need—and I mean *need*—to know *where* he is, *how* he is, and *what* he is doing. My child went *somewhere* without me. I want him back, or else I want to go with him. Oh Lord, have mercy, hear my words, count my tears, and look at my heart breaking and cracking. How can someone I gave birth to and loved all his life be gone, just like that? How can he lie so still and lifeless? How can it be that he will be buried and, from that point on, be invisible? Physically gone from my reach, from this earth? It doesn't seem possible or real. The devastating news is that it's the new reality, with or without my say. I just *can't* and *don't* believe it. How selfish of me to feel wounded, when the worst has happened to him, not me. Guilt arises.

The floor feels like a trapdoor opening up, and I feel my heart fall out of my chest, yet I feel suspended in air. I think I have stopped breathing, and with that all, time has stopped. It's like being frozen in place and time, until I free-fall to the floor, which feels like quicksand under my feet. The dead silence of denial first rushes through me.

Then my head and my mind feel as if they are cases of gunpowder and dynamite gone amok. Sparks of confusion and questions ricochet in my head.

All I can do is pace, and yet there is nowhere to go. I am pacing with no direction, but I must continue moving because it's impossible to stay still or remain in one spot. What does one do with oneself in a tragedy like this? Walking around in circles is my way of running from the truth. I want to be alone, yet I want people around me. I am in a zone, repeating furiously that this is not true. My child is *not* gone. What is this word *gone*? Are you *not* coming back? I know you would if you could. Child, why has your body stopped? You can't help it and I feel achingly sorry for you. How dare this happen to you? It's not right, it's not fair, and I feel it is criminal. Someone has to pay for this and suffer cruelly through retribution. Oh, how I don't realize it yet, but it will be me suffering a lifetime of agony from the very second my child, or anyone I love, ceases to live. Our children, our loved ones, must exist, for themselves, for us, for everybody else. I demand action!

I beg and plead for the clock to rewind. How can time be so cruel? How? Everything seems so distorted—life, reality, everything. If I am sleepwalking, please hurry and wake me up from this nightmare, and then this can go away. Someone, anyone, shake me, wake me, even hit me. Oh my God, if this is true, and I am awake, then make me sleep for a hundred years. I can't face this.

My world is crashing down around me, and who is noticing? My son's life is missing from his body. Why is the earth still revolving? Doesn't the world care? Have you ever been as lost in the chaos as I am? I feel like an outcast. I am in limbo between his life and his death. I can't find my way to him. Where is he?

My mind and my body are suffering from withdrawal. Doesn't anybody realize this? I loved my child, held him, hugged him, kissed him, nursed him through illnesses, talked to him, celebrated life with him, and now my child is not here. Don't people realize why grievers cannot eat or sleep, why we shake, why we cry uncontrollably, lose interest in life, become forgetful and suffer all the other symptoms that overwhelm us? My mind and body crave my child; it's overwhelming, physically and emotionally. People suffer from withdrawal from drugs, food, gambling, activities, and so on. People find that believable, but not when it involves loss and grief. Why is this grief so unspoken and untouchable? How can anyone in his right mind think we need to get over it and move on? Let it go? *Never!* Do you all hear me? *Never!* And if it was someone else, *he* wouldn't, either. Ever!

Now I think I know the desperation of an animal when its body is stuck in a trap. I could rip off a limb and leave it in the trap so that I could free myself and run away from this. This is happening right now, and I want to run. I want to wish this away, but I feel I cannot move. I am trapped. My heart has stopped, and yet it is beating like a wild drum. If I run as fast as I can, it won't happen, it didn't happen, fate can't catch me. *Cruel fate, chase me, but I won't let you catch me,* I think desperately. But where am I going? Am I running *from* this or am I running *to* something? Where in the world can I run to? There is no one who can change this and nowhere that I will be untouched by this. *Nowhere* stares me right in the face. I am lost, never so lost in my life. I couldn't possibly be in this nightmare. I want to protect my child; I would give up my life for him, so why is he gone? Let it be *me* instead; please, *I beg of you, me … not him.* Take this nightmare back, please. No wait, this isn't true. Seriously, it cannot be true. *Not real, not real, not real,* I repeat to myself. How can my heart still beat when it's so broken? I don't understand.

Is it understandable to say that it was a blessing to be in shock and denial for months and months in the beginning? In my mind, I honestly could not believe that this horrific fate was true. It did not resonate within my mind. My mind and heart kept saying, "This isn't true; it's a haze of confusion that is not real." It was the best way to maintain sanity during an insane experience. There was comfort in not believing and not accepting the facts. I didn't want to react and confront this shock and loss. No one wants pain, loss, and grief to become a part of them, so why have a part of it? Someone precious was taken from me, and it is unbelievable and unacceptable. I didn't ask for this; therefore, I don't want it. This seems logical; otherwise, it's much too draining. It's too brutal to face reality when it's too brutal to accept it. If I hadn't been cushioned with shock and disbelief, I would have felt that my head was going to explode. It's that bad.

I am so sad. How can a heart wrench so badly and yet feel so numb? Have you felt the same? Do you wish life would hurry on so that finally, finally, you can honestly rest in peace? I am so tired of this round and round, unhappy merry-go-round. It's a ride that never ends. This no longer seems to have had a beginning, and there is no end. I am so tired, so dizzy, so jealous of those who have not been touched by tragedy. How does it feel to be so happy-go-lucky? My child was good. Why can't the good live happily ever after, and the evil ones get what they deserve—an early death? Oh my, listen to these horrible thoughts and words. Who do I think I am anymore? I'm changing. How cruel of me to be so judgmental, but I can't help feeling this way right now. I sometimes want revenge. I often feel angry. I'm not me anymore. I feel hatred and injustice toward people and circumstances because of that day. I do not recognize myself in the mirror anymore. I am changed. What has become of me? I'm not proud that I feel so much hatred. Forgive me, I am human.

My world is crashing down around me. It feels as if nobody is noticing. My son is missing from this world, but who else is crying, besides me? I feel raw; my emotions are unspoken, indescribable, and so tender. I wouldn't want anyone to feel this wounded and hopeless. I pray you have not had to feel this way. If you have and maybe still do, my heart goes out to you in the most sincere way.

It Feels Like

It feels like an elephant is sitting on my chest. It's so difficult to breathe. I feel like I am suffocating. My son and I were such an immeasurable part of each other. He doesn't breathe, I don't breathe. He lives no more, I live no more. How can my heart race so quickly when I feel so dead? I feel like a zombie, but at the same time I can't stay still; I pace, with nowhere to go. Where can I go? There is nowhere where I can turn time back, where I can feel normal again. This is it. It's over. Time has stopped. My son's life has stopped. I have stopped. Have any of you felt the same? What can we do? No one has the answer. Honestly, I don't care anymore. I'm so tired. I can't sleep, I can't stay awake. Lightning, please strike me. Get me now, get me good! Let it be over just as quickly as my loved one was taken away. I don't care that it's a new day. I don't care that the sun is shining so warmly in the perfect blue sky. I cared too much, and now I don't care about all that anymore.

I feel invisible. Please make me invisible. How much longer must I live and endure this unbearable pain? Every breathing moment feels like a curse. Sorry, Lord, for being so unappreciative of life and the blessings that still remain in my life. I'm sorry. I don't seem strong and courageous enough to move on with my life. I am human, and this is how it is for me right now. I exist, but I do not live. This is how it feels when someone is ripped out of your life, your arms, your being. It's raw, and some people don't care to know and understand the world of grief and pain. It's too dark and dreary for them. They are afraid that it's contagious. Maybe that's why some grievers feel such isolation. We exist in a quarantine world of our own. We and our loved ones didn't ask for this. We didn't deserve it. But we have to endure it night and day, over and over again. My son breathes no more, nor do I. That's how it feels for me. I'd rather not feel anymore.

I am trying to feel the pain my child did as if it were my own. It will never compare, but I would rather feel the suffering and death for him—instead of him. It's heartbreaking that I was not there for my loved one at the accident scene. I torture myself about the last moments of his life. I pray that he was surrounded by the power and mercy of God. Surely he was not alone. We wish we could do that for our loved ones. I hate to see anyone suffer or go through trauma or sickness. Realistically, I cannot live my son's last, suffering moments, and that causes me to wail and fall with heartache. He died instantly, so I hear, but what of the seconds before the impending and shocking impact? I can't stop entwining my pain with his pain. Reliving his last moments is a self-inflicted suffering I can't seem to stop. This is a preoccupation that has evolved into a post-trauma way of life. All I can hope is that this sorrow will help me grow with more wisdom and compassion, so that I can help shape the future in a positive way.

It feels like I am standing in quicksand. It's so constricting around my stomach. If I stay still, I will sink into oblivion. I must work, pay bills, take care of others. I must move and attempt to trudge through the quicksand. I feel like I will be surrounded by quicksand the rest of my life. It will be so hard to live like this, to move so slowly and keep myself from sinking in the quicksand. I can't move up and out. I proceed slowly, constricted, but I move to keep from being swallowed up. It's going to be a long, difficult, slow process. I don't think any book or person—anything—is really going to help or save me. My belief will help me grow stronger. But right now, it's just me, at my own pace. If you feel like me, please find me. Then none of us will be alone in this difficult journey. Maybe we could carry each other, hold each other, speak our children's names over and over, and we will know in our hearts and minds that we are not crazy. We are not disillusioned. Our reaction to trauma is acceptable behavior born of an unacceptable loss.

It feels like I will appreciate roadside memorials, tributes, and anything that leaves a legacy of love more now than ever. I praise those who don't abandon their loved ones and never stop celebrating their lives. It feels like grieving will lead me to find my way home to some sort of peace and serenity. God bless all those who carry empathy, sympathy, compassion, and memories of loved ones within them. The world needs more special people like them, so I thank them now and forever.

So Alone

*T*hat's right, I feel so alone. Do you feel the same? Are you surrounded by many people but feel alone and lonely? Where is everybody? I want somebody right here with me, if you know what I mean. My child can't physically hold me anymore, and I can't do the same. I feel so cheated. I needed someone to hold me at the worst time of my life. Why won't anybody hold me now—I mean truly hold me and not let go so quickly? I crave the healing, caring touch, as soft as an angel's wing, yet as strong as God's will.

Don't worry about making me sad if you visit, because I am sad already. I am constantly thinking about my child. I want so desperately to talk about him. I am sadder when no one chooses to speak of the memories or ask about his life. I don't want to feel alone in loving and remembering him. I want my heart to be as open as the sky above. I want to share. Sometimes I want to be alone. This is a disorganized time for the mind.

Don't feel sorry for me, but find the time to listen and learn from my painful journey, so that you may learn and share it with others. We were all meant to share with each other; isn't that why we live on this earth? Aren't our deaths meant to have meaning? Can't I know why my son left us? Why? Why didn't some people in my life want to help me or learn something about this unhappy journey? These become lost chances for more bonding and new memories. This makes it all the sadder. My inner body is so bloated from anger, hatred, and pity. I feel that all that is left of me is a shell. I feel so heavy and tired. Do you ache with pain and sorrow too? All the energy that I have is the tears that run so freely. I'm not dead, but I'm not alive, either. Right now, this tragedy is defining my life. How can it be that we must adjust to living without our loved one by our side? Who knows the answer, please tell. How do I become accustomed to the hurt and the loss?

Have you lost touch with many friends and family during your tender time of mourning? Have many not called or visited following the tragedy? If they only knew how distraught we really feel and how left out we have become.

Do not condemn those of us who grieve if we do not grieve like you did. Perhaps some people don't grieve, or they avoid it, or their grieving time is shorter and less complicated. Do not judge us, because it can then alienate us and make some of us feel even more alone. Sometimes it's better if someone offers quiet support, rather than saying something unkind or hurtful. Sometimes just listening and saying nothing is enough. Just being there is everything in the world. Please, somebody be there for those of us who feel so vulnerable. It's difficult to explain that we are filled with pain and, at the same time, empty as a shell.

Sleep Nevermore

*D*oes anyone know what I mean? Nighttime, others fall asleep so easily. For me, lying in bed in the dark is like a torture chamber. I have not slept in four years. I have forgotten how to sleep. Honestly, I have forgotten how to breathe. I watch much television because it can be so mindless, until I am exhausted, sometimes till three in the morning. Then I go to bed because I must arise for work at five. I hope to pass out from exhaustion before the morning alarm rings, which would be a blessing. Instead it starts all over again—the thinking and the yearning and the tears. There is no peace. I beg for a break, but there is none.

The darkness seems to smother me. The fact is that this is mourning, and it is so wearisome to cope. Do you beg for your loved one to appear in a vision or perhaps visit in a dream? Why can't they visit us, even just once, to let us know they are all right—perhaps happy—and then we would know they are with us when we think about them or need them. It's all such a mystery. I need faith because no one here can tell me the answer. The case is never solved; I beg to believe in something, because no one here can give a definitive answer. It's a life lesson. Meanwhile, there is no sleep. How can we not have drowned in our own tears?

I don't want to forget what his voice sounded like. I try to hold on to his energy and smile. It's been too long since I saw the twinkle in his eye. It doesn't feel real. Maybe he is on a long trip. He was deployed to Afghanistan for almost a year. I can try to pretend he is away on a mission. I feel as if I am in a haze. It's wonderful to be numb sometimes. Other times, I feel consumed with hopelessness. I miss him terribly.

Nighttime has become the time I relive this horrible news. It's something about the darkness and the silence. I think about how others can fall asleep so quickly, so restfully. What is that like? I am so envious. If I lie in bed, the tears flow quickly, the thoughts never stop, the personal agony builds up, and then I feel like a trapped animal. Why even bother lying there? Why bother closing my eyes? I feel so exhausted that my head just spins. Running on empty, how long can this go on? Why have I not fainted or collapsed yet?

I have forgotten how to sleep. I lost it. I don't know if I will ever find it or get it back again. Will it ever feel the same? If I do fall asleep, why do I feel as if I fought a million battles with a wicked monster the entire time? Morning arises, and I am more tired than before. This is why I now do not want to sleep anymore. It's because I can't seem to sleep, and it feels like restless torture when it's time to rise. It's impossible to sleep with this much tension. I have never felt so fatigued in my life. Have I been sleepwalking while awake? Too much is going through my mind—past, present, and future all at once. Restless, with no peace of mind; this is my day and night. My son, my emotions, and my guts were taken from me and buried at the cemetery. This is crazy. I feel crazy.

How Did We Do It?

*H*ow did we do it? How could I stand by his casket and not jump in there with him? How do I accept the fact that I am there next to a casket holding the lifeless body of someone I truly love and who was so full of life not long before? Lifeless, I tell you. Why are the dead so still and so mysterious to us? At this point, I cannot join him and be a part of him anymore. I feel so left behind, forever. During the funeral, it was difficult to appease people with their grief when I hadn't seen or spoken to them in years. Some knew nothing about the life of my son and what had happened. Why didn't they ask me? I implore anyone to ask me so that I may share.

It's like an out-of-body experience being near the casket. For me, I can't celebrate his life when there is no life anymore. It's not like he is sleeping and breathing softly. I am so close to him but feel so far away from him. In death, people are a shell that we have never seen before and never expected to. I am powerless. He can't be woken. I can't make him move and respond as he always has. It's so scary and mysterious. I lost him. All that's left now is me and my memories. Being next to his body now, I will never get this moment again. This is the true, final good-bye to his presence. Why am I holding back tears from everyone now? They only blur my vision. I want to scream and wail. I don't know if I will ever feel whole again.

This is not enough. I want him back. There will be hell to pay for this. But right now, the fatigue, the exhaustion, the disbelief are taking me on this hellish ride. There I am, playing the part of someone who has it all together. The funeral arrangements were made, the casket chosen, the clothes picked and delivered, and anything else that needed to be done was done. What am I going to do with this undying love? There is so much noise in my head. It's like I am in two different worlds. Here and there, although at present, I don't know where here and there are. Lost dreams and promises are being taken away and buried in a casket in the ground. I must cave in to accepting what reality has taken away. What should have been was taken away and lost to this world.

Oh my God, the cemetery. How odd and unfamiliar it all was. There are no rehearsals for this kind of tragedy and experience. I didn't want a public burial. This scene looked and felt like a wound in the earth. All of it seemed so calm and peaceful and well organized, but inside of me, it did not feel like that. The rainbow was taken with my loved one. I wanted privately to be there and scream and tear the dirt away. I wanted to sleep on the dirt the entire night to keep my child warm and safe. I didn't want to leave him alone there. How did I leave with all the people and go back to the house? Why did I worry about whether there was enough food for everyone and whether they were comfortable? Listening to others' conversations about what they were planning to do the upcoming weekend, catching up on each other's lives … it was torturous, but I did it. I resented it. I wanted to scream, "My child is dead. Why are we alive, why are we talking, and how we could have left him back at the cemetery?" What do I care what anybody's plans are or how work is going for them? It's not what is important at this moment. We should be lying on the floor, kicking and screaming, and chanting "No! No! No!" All I want to do is cry and cry and cry. Why won't anyone let me scream and cry? I wail silently inside, and it's painful and raw. Let me show you how I really feel, please? Show me how you really feel, please? I feel as if a spell were cast on me, and I feel invisible.

Then, the day after the funeral, where is everybody? The week after the funeral—months, years—I ached with a full heart for my child. Doesn't anyone want to see his picture, gaze at his military awards, and know about the young children he left behind? Do you remember where he was buried? Won't you want to leave a little something at the gravesite, blow a gentle kiss at the tombstone? Never mind, I will do those things and more. I will do it for me and for everyone else. I will do it for me and for him. God is with him now, and that's what is most important and special. My deceased parents are with him. Take care of each other, my departed loved ones. I am eternally grateful for that.

I never thought I would be experiencing, let alone writing, about the cause and effect of devastation of the mind, body, and spirit because of the death of a child. We can take so much for granted, and we underestimate the impact of loss of life when it doesn't touch us personally. When we become front and center to this statistic, how we live through it is unpredictable.

How did I go back to work after this? I was a walking earthquake, a tidal wave, but I needed to act so acceptingly silent about it all. That's how everyone wants it because it's more socially acceptable this way. It's so frustrating and unfathomable that I conformed to this way. I must work, shop, and act as if I am in one piece, presentable to everyone, every time, everywhere. Back in the day, mourners wore black for a year. How are we allowed to show our grief and misery in this day and age? I doubt that many individuals would want to witness personal breakdowns or to try to understand them. It's sad, and it's not fair.

Something Happens to You

Something happens to you when you hear the news that your child has died. It began when my son was not returning my phone calls that treacherous day. It ended when I received that fatal phone call, which changed my life forever. Something happens to you when you view your loved one's lifeless body, eyes forever closed. How did I choose a casket, a funeral home, obtain a medical examiner's report, make plans, and demonstrate strength in public? Something really happens to you when you see the hole in the ground and see the casket being lowered. You cannot go back to the way you were, *ever*.

Something happens to you when you go to the cemetery. I cannot say "visit" the cemetery. To me, a visit is a willing action. A visit is usually voluntary and something to plan and look forward to. I *want* to visit my son and for him to be alive. Going to the cemetery is something I *must* do. Does anyone really want to feel that ache in the pit of their stomach and the impending tears when they pull into the cemetery entrance? Actually, it begins a block away from the entrance gates. The cemetery is where I want to go when I want to be near his physical body. It's sick. Don't you understand that I still need his physical presence? I know that he's not there, that he is a happy soul, and he is everywhere, in heaven with God and also beside his loved ones here on earth. I can hear everyone tell me those things, but at this time, the cemetery is where I need to go. If I could dig my way down there and lie in the coffin with him, I would! It's hard to figure out what to do when the people we build our lives around are taken away so quickly. What happens next? It's a wave of shock and denial, uncontrollable tears, rawness and sorrow.

I go through the motions of the day, but nothing feels real. I may seem normal on the outside, but inside I am falling apart. I struggle with a missing chunk of my heart. Grief is so painful, so painful. It's a shadow that always follows me. I am disoriented from this crisis because it is such a major event. I crave the beauty and calmness of healing.

I have changed. I used to love the warmth of the sun and the summer. Now I crave winter, for all is frozen, and that is now how I like it. Winter symbolizes frozen in place like my heart. I am mystified about whether there was a gap between my son's last living breath and the second he died so violently in that crash. I can't help but dwell on and debate this thought. There is too much confusion, which is why it's easier to be frozen. Feeling frozen is being numb enough to survive all of this. If I move or melt, it will be painful, and I will have to feel. Can't I stay hard, sturdy, and strong? If I bend, I might break, and it will hurt. It's too much work even to move.

Fire-Breathing Dragon

*D*eath is not simple. With the loss of a loved one, many must deal with traffic accident reports, sicknesses and hospitals, victimization due to crime, wills and estates, extended family members, the law, injustice, characters involved with the death, lack of respect for the deceased, ungrateful and greedy survivors, and so on. How can individuals properly grieve with love and remembrance when untidy, shameful circumstances plague the death and the honor of their loved one? It's not just the grieving but everything else involving the death and the aftershock that is difficult and frustrating.

How can I sometimes feel like an empty shell, and other times like a fire blazing out of control? Who am I anymore? I don't recognize myself in the mirror. No one must know my private hell; they will think I am crazy. Why do I care what others think? Why? Families lose so much when they lose one of their own, especially if that person is a child, no matter how old the child is when he or she died. Maybe someday I will revel in my son's memory. I hope to appreciate life and all it has to offer. I did before this. But I've now endured more than three years of his absence. I find it difficult to write, let alone say, the dead word? I choose to say that I "lost" my son instead.

It's difficult to share the fact that I have not moved forward very much. Anger and hatred flare in every core of my existence. I want retribution. This is not fair. Have I grown from this experience? I feel as if I have shrunk. My son has lost years with his children. My son and his children were cheated, and it's not fair. I accept that this lifetime may not fulfill our dreams, but must my child lose his dreams and die so young? I lost half of me. How am I still here, walking around half-alive and half-dead? My son had so much love for so many of us. Thinking about that hurts. How do I begin to be happy with a broken heart?

When loose ends are kept hanging for some families, when questions are not answered, truth is not told, justice is not evident, deceit is evident, there is no peace, serenity, or tranquility. If circumstances do not make sense, one may question and speculate and judge and become angry and furious. I pray to sustain myself and find my own way out of this. I think of my son, and all I wish for is peace in order to emulate his life. God forgives. I am trying to work on that, because blame is a terrible way to deal with anger and everything that follows. When I feel stronger, I will try not to let negativity get the best of me. That's not who I am or what should become of me. But I feel so raw, so scorched, and so heartbroken; I can't think or see straight. One of my most important relationships has ended because of a sudden and tragic death; I am knocked to the ground.

Shame on Them

It's not easy to say shame on anyone who inflicts negativity and pain, intentionally or unintentionally, on those who are grieving. Either way, it can hurt fragile individuals. This is a time when a broken and tender heart can become hard with rage, anger, and lack of forgiveness. As survivors of a lost loved one, people may not intend to wake up and may choose to hate those who cause turmoil during this heartbreak. Brokenhearted people need empathy and sincerity and honor. This is my opinion. It is sad that many families break apart when a loved one dies, when the death should be a bond that enables them to grow stronger. Some families, thankfully, pull together and grow.

Is it harsh to feel like this? Losing anyone in your family or anyone you care about provokes feelings of sadness and longing. People feel and show their emotions in different ways. Sadly, some people appear heartless to those around them. It hurts to feel abandoned by and isolated from those around us, just at the time we need them most. Any indifference adds to the personal pain already festering in the brokenhearted.

Allowing others in the family to remember and honor the loved one and his or her contributions is an acknowledgment of love. To do otherwise would be so sad. Life moves on quickly for some, but slowly and meticulously for others. It's difficult not to pass judgment when we witness various circumstances which we cannot control.

I would hope that death would be treated with dignity and respect. Questions—especially those of children and other family members—should be answered, so they are prepared for present and future encounters with life and death. Any misinformation or dishonesty can cause everlasting damage. People need to talk to each other honestly, openly, and earnestly. I hope people are able to express themselves freely and not be judged or mocked. Just because someone doesn't fall apart or break down in a dramatic way doesn't mean they have recuperated from their loss.

Children and Other Family Members

Wouldn't it be wonderful to gift children and family members with positive memories of their loved one? Children who lost a parent to war, illness, an accident, etc., could be made to feel like they knew their parent, even if they never had the chance to. In a hopeful world, loved ones will never be replaced or forgotten. Photographs, counseling, discussions, and family members may help to bring balance to children during this traumatic time.

If children and family express their grief, they can share their memories and feel connected to their loved ones and to the loved one who died. One hopes that grief is portrayed positively; otherwise the wounds are kept open because grief must be kept hidden. Fun times are great, but not if they are used to cover up an enormous emotion. Perhaps wounds would heal and not fester privately and painfully if individuals had the opportunity to speak of the deceased freely and openly. Adequate support can teach effective coping skills. If people need to be together, one hopes that they can be. This is my opinion. Many people do not want to be forgotten or left out of other people's lives. It's sad to see this happen to many families at such a delicate time. It's beautiful, on the other hand, to see people come together for meaningful times of remembrance and a future of promise. I feel there is so much beauty and diversity in this world, and for me, it would mean the world to share it with loved ones and in the memory of loved ones.

It's Not the Same, and There's No Turning Back

The loss of a child, no matter what age, is difficult to compare to the death of any other loved one. Some may say they know how it feels; they have lost someone other than a child. Some can try to imagine; I used to do that "before," but that's all it was—imagination and speculation. When it really happens, there is no going back from imagining. All is not okay, and it never will be; it will never be as it was. Once it happens, your child's death is set in stone, literally and figuratively. There is no bargaining. It is done and always will be. No going back except for memories. There will never be a physical touch, a conversation, a look into each other's eyes. There will be *nothing forevermore*. We cannot settle for anything, for there *is no choice*. Their future and our future with them are gone. Children should outlive their parents, not the other way around.

We can turn around in circles a million times, but nothing can change the mortifying fact of our loved one's death. How merciless is this? It is a fact. It becomes a statistic—a finality—with no possibility of turning back. It feels like injustice, but it is the circle of life, whether caused randomly, by fate, or otherwise. From the beginning of time until the end of time, sorrow and death are a part of life. Nothing will ever be the same for the people who knew and loved their departed. I can try all types of thoughts in my fantasies, but the loss must be coped with in reality. No matter where I go or what I do, I feel as if I carry my hell with me. My vision is blurred by tears, and the world is colorless to me. There is barely any light, laughter, joy, warmth; all were gone in an instant, and my colorless world seems to linger forever.

Afterward

*W*here do I go from here? No one knows what is waiting for me around the corner. If life was this cruel to my child, sock it to me, then! I can take it. I am so numb, so lost; I don't care if the ground opens up to take and swallow me. I don't care if an airplane crashes upon me. Lightning: hit me with your best shock. Whatever it may be, I weep, I am here, come and get me; it can't be soon enough.

I took a trip and I bought a hot tub. I thought these actions would fill the hole in my life and help me feel complete in some way. I realized that nothing can mend a broken heart. It's all just a temporary Band-Aid. I was seeking happiness of sorts, but that road seems crumbled *at this point*. Time is not on my side right now.

I feel so small and powerless. Breathing is such a struggle; where is the energy and optimism to do anything else? The tears are nonstop. Wouldn't it be great if, when the tears dry up, the pain and agony also dry up and disappear? There is no bartering to relieve or erase what is in my heart and in my mind.

Fate, you can take my son away from me, but you can't take him away from my heart and mind. Do you hear me?

In time, I will need to get used to this pain, or I will go crazy. There are no shortcuts in life; I need to face it and feel it. Is this my lesson in life—tolerance or acceptance of pain and loss? Right now, sadness and loss are taking over my mind. They are affecting everything I see, feel, and do. I cry, and nobody knows how much time I spend doing it. I don't mean to be self-absorbed, but grief is such hard work, and it hurts. I didn't ask for any of this to happen. I want to continue loving my child without hurting so badly. As a living being, I crave peace, serenity, harmony, love, security, hopefulness, and well-being. I wished those things upon my son-fostered them in his life-and I felt those things because of him. He's not here anymore, yet I continue to look for him. Without hope, I feel hopeless. Now I resort to being the best dreamer I know; it's more bearable that way.

Expecting Too Much

*A*m I wrong, Son, to expect so much from you? I want to ask you to visit me in my dreams. I want to feel your presence all the time. I want as many signs from you as possible. Should I respect your freedom from this world and let you be in peace? Perhaps the plan is for you to do mighty things somewhere else. I should let you go. Is it your turn to let me go to spread my wings toward a new way of life? The problem is that I won't let you go. I want you back. I can't? Then I want some part of you to be here with me. I need you, Son. Yes, I am supposed to be the grown-up. I am expected to adjust, acclimate, and move on. I apologize for expecting too much. Call me selfish, but also call me loving and devoted! Can I still get my wishes, though? Please?

Too many days are passing without my loved one. When is that painful lump in my throat going to disappear? It seems like so long ago when I was happy; now that feels like another lifetime and like I was another person. Where am I? Where did I go? I expected too much in this life. Now my fortune has shifted away, like sand in an hourglass that has suddenly upturned. Why didn't anyone warn me that we live to die?

Lost Expectations

My expectations are killing me second by second. I want what I can't have, and I cannot control what I want. A loved ones death might not be an isolated incident because others might be a part of that fateful day. Wouldn't we want those people to reach out to us first? We would hope to hear how sorry others were and that they think of our lost one every day. Whether it's planting a tree in our loved one's honor or placing a flower at the site, any gesture would be cherished by a grieving family member. My son was so much more than a deployed soldier, a veteran, a loving family member. He was here, and he was important in many lives. It's important for me to find accountability from this devastation. I care; therefore I fly quite a distance to put flowers and statues at the site.

I had hoped and expected that the investigation would be compassionate and would issue a just report accompanied by just actions. I had hope that any persons involved that fateful day would also be emotionally involved. What am I to expect? Why do I feel a sense of judge and jury? I cannot control anyone or anything. I realize, painfully, after three torturous, angry, resentful years, that expectations are senseless and painful. All these feelings have compounded my sadness. It was slowly eating me alive, turning me into a fire-breathing dragon filled with anger, resentment, and sadness. Emotional thoughts consumed me endlessly. People are people, but I am I. I will find my own way to view life and events.　.

I've learned not to expect anything from anyone. I cannot control anyone. I am powerless over others. I am slowly empowered to learn that I can only deal with *my* feelings and *my* actions. Thank you, my son, for teaching me this lesson.

Why Is He Missing His Life?

$\mathcal{I}$t was cut so short. In my eyes, there was so much more for him to do in this life. He was such an extraordinary person who helped others. So many individuals counted on him for so much. He was a soldier who served his country. So many could have learned and benefited from his actions. He was an optimist who accepted what life had to offer and made the best of everything. He was to watch his daughters grow and be a part of their present and future. He was an older brother who was supposed to be there to share a long life with his younger sibling and other family members. I was supposed to die knowing they would take care of each other without me. Life is now fractured, and, just like ants, we scurry to do the best to survive in the face of what we find in front of us. Why is he missing his life, so soon, so unexpectedly?

I can scream, "Why did this happen to my loved one?" knowing it happens to others and will continue to do so. No one can promise us a perfect and just life. Sadly, to those who have loved and survived, it can be a road of pain and sorrow. I hope that someday wonderful memories will replace the pain.

I miss him so much, but I feel even sadder for him. As far as I know, we have only one life here. He didn't get to live until a ripe, old age and experience all that life has to offer. Who knows what choices he would have made and the life he would have experienced? I should feel grateful for the time he had, but honestly, selfishly, I feel he was cheated. I feel he was a worthwhile individual who deserved more than what happened that fateful day. I am not ready to accept this reality. What are you doing with your abundance of feelings and lost hope? Please share it if you can, I want to know. Some of us need to know. Please help. Tell us.

My son accepted me the way I was. I yearn now to do as he did and accept the way things are and who I am because of it. It feels like invisible wires are tangled in my body, and the connection has gone haywire, and the feed to the energy is zapped. Are you also in need of repair?

There is more love in this world because of him. His family and friends spread his love and their own love daily. He continues to live through how we carry our relationship with him and with others within us, but I wish his life had not ended. That is what makes it so sad. There were so many things yet for my departed to do, say, and experience. I am the one left to ponder it all. I am glad he experienced the joys and blessing that life had to offer, and perhaps now he sees and feels something better than the sun. I believe it is the eternal light.

Say His Name, I Sing

*W*hat is wrong, everyone? He had just died, and I rarely heard his name spoken aloud!

I know he's no longer here, but I so want to feel him near. *Say his name.* I just want to hear his name.

For those who've loved and lost, you know it's a heavy cost. Don't you want to hear your child's name over and over again?

The funeral was crowded. Now the people are gone, and where is everyone now?

Where have you been since then? I still exist, I still persist—no calls, no mentioned memories, no time to spend anymore with us mourners, no nothing? I just want to hear my son's name. *Say his name.*

He was a hero, a soldier, but he did not survive a motorcycle ride a few blocks from his home. I tried his phone many times before he left our world; no answer. I called his name; no answer. Yes, I still call his name; I'll never stop calling his name. There is still no answer.

It breaks my heart. I can't help but fall apart.

Please talk and share. I need someone to care; it's important to me. Please don't be unwilling; open up and you'll see that it's easy to say his name.

I want to hear your name, Son. People other than me, please say it. Everybody, please say it.

Grief is a life sentence of despair; I wish for others to spend more time to care. I haven't slept since he died; day and night I've cried.

I can't believe you are not here. I want to go where you are, no matter how far. I sometimes don't care what I leave behind; I'm going out of my mind.

But for now, while I'm here, I want to say your name out loud for everyone to hear. It's what makes you feel near, and each letter is filled with tears … of longing and remembering.

Oh Lord, I'm so grateful he was in my life. I despise the word *was*; it means not now, not today. It means not anymore. Forever is a death sentence to me. Why did this have to be?

Life moves on, but we raw, unspoken, grieving folks go out of our minds. Can't think, can't focus, I feel so left behind. It's difficult to catch up to everyone else who is keeping up with life; life can be so unkind.

Son, your children almost too young to remember you as Dad, it's too sad. As for me, what does every parent want to hear, what do they hold so dear? It's their child's name. This is how it is when our world is torn apart, it feels so dark.

I need to hear his name. Everyone—someone—say his name with love, honor, and treasured remembrance.

Say our children's names, say them, we want to hear them, to be near them, never to fear them, always to believe in them; they're so strong, so right ... the names still have vigor, still have a fight ... their beautiful, never-ending names ... *say his name, say her name, say their names* ... please?

My Child Would Want Me To …

*M*any parents can complete that phrase. My child was a twenty-five year-old father, caring son, brother, and friend, a veteran of war. He always wanted me to be happy. He would want me to laugh and act as if I have not a care in the world. I am not like that. If I had died suddenly, my son would have gone to a party the following week if he had been invited. That is the way he was. He loved me so much, and he would have carried that love throughout his life, and he would have lived his life happily and to the fullest.

If he has been watching the past three years, he would be shaking his head at my state of mind. He wouldn't want me to feel so burdened. This unbearable sadness makes me feel as if I must carry the weight of time on my shoulders; yet I want to learn and grow from this.

If I had known I would lose my child so soon, I would still have given birth and loved him. No regrets. To have loved and experienced his life was such a gift; I don't care how much I hurt now. My agony is worth the love I gave and received from him. Stab me a million times over; I want his life here again. Aren't your memories of your loved one more precious than gold? Is there a lesson in this? When we ourselves are gone, we would want others to live life as fully as possible. I would never want anyone to put themselves into a box of hell. Why can't I practice what I preach?

My child would want me to experience joy and to cry less. He would want me to grab hold of life as quickly as possible after his absence. He would expect me to redirect my life in a positive and happy direction. I need to listen to his everlasting messages of love.

Maybe He's Like That

I've researched near-death experiences where individuals talk about the bright light, the tunnel, the overwhelming beauty, the unconditional love, the warmth, the overall sense of peace and well-being, and the desire not to return to life.

Maybe my son is like that. Maybe he felt no fear; maybe his soul left his body before the horrific crash. Maybe he feels happy and loved. Maybe he now understands what his purpose was here in this temporary life and the accomplishments he should be proud of. Maybe he is in such a good place, he doesn't feel those negative earthly feelings that we do. Rather, he feels only love and care, he wishes us the best, and he is comforted that we will all be reunited.

Maybe my son is like that, and he can see and be with everyone he loves and everyone who loves him at any time. Wow, what a great power and gift that would be. I think of watching an ant crawl to a grape or a crumb a few feet away. The ant doesn't see the long journey and the dangers that can be encountered. This tiny living creature just hauls along to get what it needs. We are the same, I guess. We cannot foresee how difficult and long the journeys in our lives are. We still plow away to get what we need, and we reap rewards along the way, for as long as we have the time to do it. We have limitations, but we continue to haul away.

But for my departed loved one, I can believe, I can speculate, I can fantasize. Maybe he is like that, and it's now better and more beautiful for him than I can ever realize. Better there than here. This would make me feel so much better for him. Be at ease, my son, and rest in peace. As for me, maybe I can be like that someday and feel some sort of peace and contentment here on earth, as I journey through my life. How I can find it and live it, who knows, but maybe I can be like that too. I hope so. If I can be so loving and loyal to the one I miss so terribly, I owe him and myself this legacy of strong will.

This Is Not Over

I will never let you go. We are a part of each other. If you lived in another state or country, I would survive because I would know you are alive and well. I would worry all the time, but there would be peace within me, knowing you were still living your life. You may be "gone" in the physical sense, but I refuse to let this be over. I am a bit stronger now, and I will not let this relationship be over. I will promise myself to keep this relationship going and growing stronger. The burden is on me, but I owe it to us. I believe that it will be reciprocal.

I believe that death should not erase the past with anyone we have known and loved. There should be a place in our hearts for our loved ones, so that love can continue. Love is comforting and healing and is power here on earth. No, this is not over, Son.

This is not over, you and I. I cannot speak for others who love you, but I will never let you go. You are my past, and I will continue to share the present and future with you. I have to, because I love you and miss you so much. People, I think you may be doing the same. We shouldn't feel ashamed to grieve, because we are feeling the love.

About all the tears I have wept, I will not feel any shame. Reliving memories, missing what the future could have brought, all this is our love continuing to flow. It's not over, and I never want it to be. How about you? How do you do it?

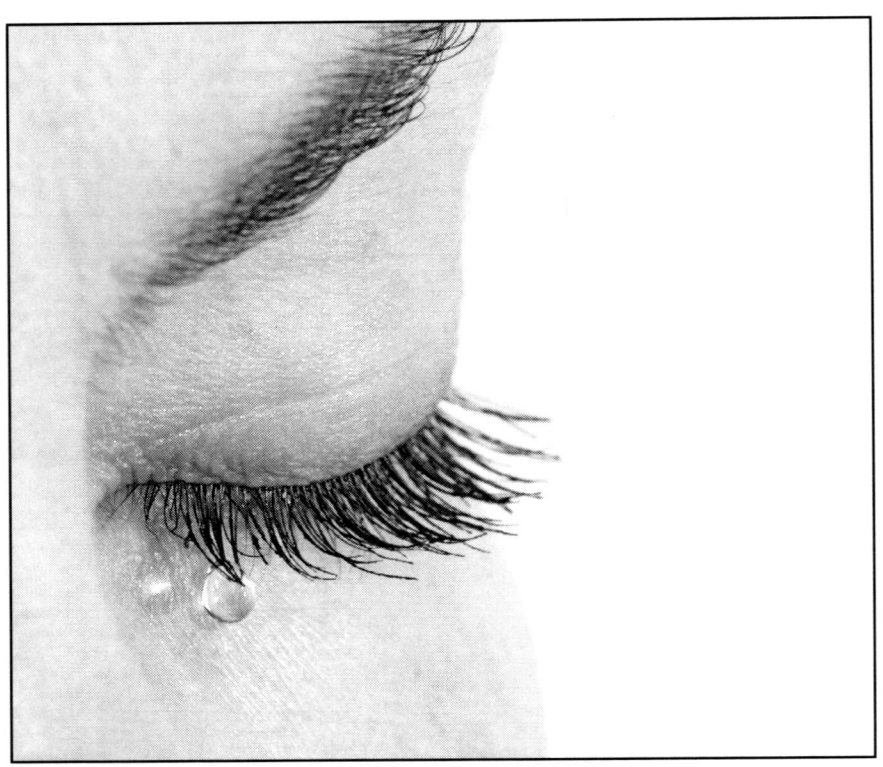

Silent Pain

*I*t has become a silent pain. The outside world, the people I know and see; they may not want to witness the agony and the personal pain of others. It may be uncomfortable for them to view and understand. I may be judged. There is no choice but to adapt myself to the norms of outwardly and socially accepted behavior. I must withdraw my rawness inward. I carry it silently, as it sears deeper and deeper into my soul. No one knows the chaos and the screaming and crying from within. This entire experience is unimaginable until you live through it.

Many individuals think we are fine or recovered because we are composed and functional. "Falling apart" would definitely cause others to feel uncomfortable or withdraw from our presence. It takes much emotional energy to work and carry on conversations and maintain relationships. I'm telling you, this is true. If I were not in this situation, I would never have known and felt this, let alone understood it. People feel emotionally spent and disorganized in situations like moving, divorcing, losing a home, etc. Imagine the walk of grief and sorrow. The walk is painful and everlasting. Grief and anger are exhausting. Do you feel as if you are constantly fighting back tears?

I'm not daydreaming about an exotic vacation while I am quietly driving, working, shopping, or involved in a conversation with someone. I am reliving the first moment of the most horrible news imaginable. I am imaging the fatal accident scene. I am feeling the rawness of everything over and over again. I disbelieve the experience of the viewing and funeral. I am reliving the shock that my son is lifeless—physically gone from this world. All these thoughts can be wrapped up in one second in my mind.

How do we do it? How do we get up and get dressed, cook, fill out important forms, socialize, work, study, read, plan events, when all of this turmoil and pain is searing into our bodies 24-7? I want the weeping willow tree to weep over me. Let me feel the hard and soft of nature provide shelter for me and whisper its wisdom and history of withstanding time. Time seems to slow down. My boy's face, his name, will never wash from my heart. How long has it been without him? The seconds, minutes, days, nights, and all of time are cloudy in this mysterious world without him.

I will not be ashamed that I miss my child and that I still grieve so deeply. I have a broken heart, and yet I still walk with it in pieces. I can cry without tears falling from my eyes. I can walk, even though I feel like I have broken ribs, which makes every breath hurt so badly. All hope seems to be faded. I feel anxiety and anger, and yet when I think about my child, I melt into tenderness and caring. It's so hard and heavy to become a cornucopia of all these things. How do we do it? It cannot be explained. The longer the time since his death, the worse it feels for me, not just mentally but also physically. It's worse because more time has lapsed since the time we had together on this earth. For me, the longer the absence, the more it hurts.

Grieving may be a way of maturing in the most difficult way possible, but learning to make it invisible to others is excruciating. It's like death all over again. I resent hiding my grief, no matter how long it lasts, because I feel I am cheating my child and myself. I am making him die all over again, and I am dying little by little every time I cover my sadness. It should not be wrong, especially when it is so honest! Don't people realize how impossible it feels to embark on a new life, when the past one is shattered? The life of our loved one is missing from our piece of the pie. You wouldn't accept that from a bakery or pizza shop. How dare the business give us an incomplete pie? It's illegal, unethical, and unimaginable. It's crazy! And yet we live and breathe, second by second, without that irreplaceable, priceless piece of our departed. The piece missing is not smooth, people, it has jagged edges. It hurts so much. I didn't even have a chance to say good-bye. Maybe that's why I can't let go.

What Am I Supposed to Do from Now till the End of Time?

*W*hat are mourners supposed to do from now on? I will miss my child and all my lost loved ones until the moment I take my last breath. What are we supposed to do? There will never be enough counseling or love from others or medicine or busywork to fill in or get rid of the void and the heartache that many of us carry within ourselves.

Son, all I can do is try to make a promise to you that my relationship with you will never end. Physically, you cannot be here. If you could, you would. I will therefore keep you with me in every way possible. I won't be impractical. I will be realistic and functional in every way possible. I can still talk to you—out loud, if I want to, or I can do so quietly. I can imagine you by my side and imagine you happy in heaven or helping anyone in need here on earth or somewhere up above. You still live, somehow and some way and somewhere. Your energy and beauty are too much for anyone to deny your constant growth and impact on others. Your energy and soul are immortal. I promise to try to live life the best I can so that you will be proud of me. Someday we will be in each other's arms, and I can look into your beautiful eyes, and you will know that I have carried on somehow; but I carried on graciously because you were by my side.

Those of us who hurt, can we promise to help each other along the way? We *can* find each other. Just as soldiers have that look and recognize each other in their brotherhood, we can too. We may find each other in the supermarket line or at a party. We are strangers, but if we share our hearts, we find that we are kindred spirits who have wearily walked the same path. The unmentionable tragedy has marked our souls. There is no fairness in any of this, but we can understand each other with compassion. I yearn to feel soft again. Will these ragged edges smooth away from wind, storm, sand, and everything else? What will you do to be soft again?

Not Just Me

$\mathcal{A}$ll people, from the beginning to the end of time, have suffered and will suffer pain and loss and heartache. We spend our lives chasing happiness, but does anyone inform us during childhood to be prepared to feel these earthly feelings of despair, loss, and anguish? Not really. Perhaps if I had been forewarned as a young child, I would have realized that these feelings of bereavement are normal and that they are an expected response to unexpected and unwanted facets of life. Do we prepare for those events in life, or do those events prepare us for life? I feel so alone, yet I'm sure I'm not alone. Perhaps other people feel the same. Where are all of you? How do we find each other in this chaos and heal each other ever so tenderly? Do all of us, at some time, focus on the day our child died, when it seems fairer to focus on the life he or she lived?

There is so much more for us to say about our deepest thoughts and feelings. I hope we begin or continue to share our raw and unspoken selves to each other and for each other. Let us be the shoulders to cry on, the fences to lean on, and that *someone* to each other. In this, may others learn what to say and what not to say to others during these tumultuous times? May our children learn from us to grieve naturally and in their own time frame so they may never suffer unresolved sadness and yet forever remember their loved ones? Real strength is the courage to face one's feelings head-on because there is no perfect world.

Time Goes On ...

*A*nother holiday goes by. People are laughing and celebrating. The birds are singing. The sun shines warmly and glowingly. Everything seems to move on. But you, my love, are buried in the ground. Your life ended. I cannot speak for others, but it seems to me, even after all this time, that I have been stopped dead in my tracks. I cannot stop thinking about you. At this time, I cannot rejoice in your childhood or the last wonderful years that you were in my life. I cannot find enjoyment in your memory just yet. All I can think about is the last moment of your horrifying accident. All I can think about is you lying in the coffin in an unthinkable and unbelievable predicament. It still seems unreal to me. Anyone else would say something is wrong with me not to have accepted this by now. I say to them, "Would *you* accept your child lying lifeless in a coffin and then buried underground for the rest of *your* life?" That's right, let them think I am crazy, but perhaps they may stop to think about it for a fleeting moment. Then, grateful and relieved, they realize that the nightmare is not their reality. They do not have to live and die with our reality. I know I can't get back the cherished life that I lost forever. I can't erase the lonely and never-ending nights, but time goes on, and so must I.

Is This a Journey?

At this raw and unspoken time, do the bereaved really believe they are heading toward a life of enthusiasm and purposeful direction? Does it feel like we are healing and growing when we bury our confused and aching head in our trembling hands? It seems more like a long and difficult process. If this is a journey, I have no direction right now. Every second is different in personal feeling and mood. It's a time of personal change and confusing development. It's a time that forces me to question life and death, and it's a time to survive continuous days and endless nights.

I am not attempting to improve or go on any self-healing trip; I am attempting to survive in a world I want to stop just for me and my missing child. No, I cannot say the d-e-a-d word. It's ugly, it's too final, and it's unimaginable and unfathomable. What on earth are we here for? I have so many questions, and no one has the right answers. Why did my child die? Why do some families fall apart? Why am I so unhappy? Why do others go through this unscathed? Why are some families the lucky ones who are never touched by pain and sorrow? My goodness, no wonder we can't focus and concentrate. Some people think we are grieving too long. *They are wrong!* Didn't they read some of the questions we are processing? Some of us are in deep thought, questioning and confused, all the while missing and grieving and coping. Grieving can seriously affect our concentration level.

When I heard the news that my son's accident was fatal, I felt as if I were lifted by a tornado that lasted months and months. Imagine a dog chasing its tail over and over; imagine the never-ending loop of a tape on a videocassette. That was my mind-set. Over and over again I replayed the accident, that curse of fate. It didn't feel like I was on a journey of self-healing. I felt I was going nowhere fast, with zero energy and stamina. How did I continue standing so shell-shocked? It happened over and over again. But I can tell you this: it couldn't go on like that forever. Sooner or mostly later, my body, mind, and spirit become exhausted and weak. It felt like a total collapse and surrender. Even a well-built machine can't go on forever. That feeling of being a flightless bird, the feeling of everything being twisted together, made it seem like nothing made sense. We are human and can only take so much.

How did everything get done? Somehow people are able to choose a coffin, speak to a funeral director, and deal with people when they just wanted to bury ourselves in a hole. Somehow they are able to stand at the cemetery with a closed coffin, knowing their once alive and energetic miracle is inside, motionless. How did they prevent themselves from collapsing at the cemetery? I look back, and I can't believe I went through all that. It must have been an out-of-body experience, because I was so numb and robotic, I don't recall much at all. And believe it or not, this must have been the beginning of my journey to healing, so to speak, and I didn't realize it. What else could it be? I can't get used to this trauma. All I can do is sometimes distance myself as an observer and repeat, "What just happened, and how in the world could I have gone through it and survived it?"

I can follow through with family, friends, doctors, counselors, medicines, etc. but it is my own personal path to crawl or to walk. No one can do it for me. Jesus had help on the way to His crucifixion.

He had His father's love, but He alone bore the burden. I think about that. It is my private and personal pain, and it's a journey I alone must do. Perhaps in time I can reach serenity, growth, understanding, and hope. Everything I need may already be within me; I just need to dig in and hold on to it. The undying love for my child can perhaps give me the strength to heal and be inspired to live once again. I can't buy hope or rejuvenation. Let me hold on to everything I love about my child so he may always be with me. Let me wish for the sadness to be replaced by precious memories.

How can it be that I must adjust to the pain and loss? This tragedy feels as if it defines my life. Society expects us to acclimate and adjust to events. If animals can tolerate a changed environment, shouldn't I be as strong and capable? Even plants adapt and change according to what nature provides. Perhaps I have much to learn from nature. Perhaps I can also keep my sense of order from my religious beliefs. There is so much to learn in life. There truly is much to cherish if only I could lift my head from the heaviness of sorrow.

Conclusion

I can't have what I want—the return of my son. I must cope in learning to continue my love for him in a nonphysical and therefore unreachable way. I need to learn to find room for the pain and sorrow to coincide with the continuation of my life. I don't have the answers or solution to this journey. What I do have is the experience of anguish at the tragic news and its immediate and long-lasting effects. It was originally an outward rawness, but it is ever so slowly seeping inward. I may be out and about more than before, and my eyes might not be as red and the look on my face may not appear as devastated. But the pain and sadness are turning inward like a sore that is closing up. Believe me, it is there and will always be there. The rawness has grown increasingly inward. But alas, my hurt has formed into these words and is no longer unspoken.

A Heartfelt Message

Dearest Son,

You are in my mind, body, and soul. I must have a new relationship with you now. It won't be in an earthly way, because it can't. What others take for granted when they stop over for a visit with their loved one, or when they make a phone call or write an e-mail, I cannot. It will never work that way again.

Now is a new way of life—no choice. My relationship with you *will* continue and will grow. I have to believe you are happy and at peace. I have to be strong. I don't want to disappoint you. I want to keep your legacy alive. You were here, and you were important. Your energy never left and continues to help others.

I can talk to you anytime I please, and you can hear me more now than ever. You are a spirit who sees me, feels me, and can be with me at any time. This way is more than anyone can ever ask for.

I can share thoughts with you without ever speaking aloud.

I must learn to live without our actual hugs, looks, voices, and touch. We are at a higher level now. Just as I believe in God, and I bask in his spiritual presence, I will learn to raise my senses to a higher level for you and with you.

I will work on changing my aching yearning for you to a feeling of peace and love. Just as a butterfly works diligently to break out of its cocoon; I have this journey to travel for as long as I have to live.

I know you want me to live life and love life. As of now, I feel no hope. I am not much interested in life. Perhaps now you can help me more than you ever have before.

May this message float on angel wings toward you. Son, please be patient with me. Don't let my sorrow keep you from your next mission.

I will never forget you. I love you.

Love,

Your mom

A Visit to My Son

It's been too long since my last visit with you, my son. I'm coming to visit you.

It's been on my mind most of the time—this is true.

I so look forward to seeing your sneaky smile and light hair.

I never know what to expect; I can't help but stare.

I'm so proud of you! When you were younger, you were such a spitfire.

You were adventurous, always trudging in muck and mire.

But you've grown up to be a wonderful young man.

You were always strong in your actions, and you stuck to your plan.

You became so independent at such a young age.

I never knew what to expect, a surprise on every page.

Who can believe that you joined the army, married, and became the father of two beautiful girls?

Both daughters share blonde hair, one with straight hair and the other one with slight curls.

I know how much you love the hot sun and riding on your motorcycle, revving so loud.

When you rode by, it surely attracted a crowd.

I dreamed about what else will become of you. Your aspirations were always high, my determined child.

You are strong willed and steadfast but empathetic and mild.

If I could go back in time, I would hug you tighter. I would hold you longer.

I would never want to let go, just want to hold you stronger.

I would want you to stay young forever! Is that every mother's dream?

But life goes on; isn't that the way it would seem?

I never worried about my care in old age. I knew I could always depend on you.

You would make sure I was comfortable and happy—this I know to be true.

I knew you would want to take good care of me. I knew you would always want your children to see me and love me anytime I care to.

I love your children; they are a part of you!

Today, on my way to visit you, I think of how worried I was back when you were deployed to Afghanistan. You had such minimal contact with the outside world.

I worried about you, and I worried you might not make it home. But you did, my son.

Your deployment was over, you are our hero, and our admiration weighs a ton!

I wish I had part of your energy and determination. I truly admire you. You are an inspiration to me.

You are a true American, a veteran, an inspiration for all to see.

I can't wait to see you. I pull up and park the car. Why am I nervous to be around the person I love so much? For a parent, it's never enough.

The drive felt long; the desperation to see you is tough.

I have new decorations for you. I can't help it. You are my firstborn; I can't help but spoil you.

The weather doesn't matter, storms or sky blue.

I have arrived! A visit to my son!

I close the car door and walk down the path. My stomach is familiarly churning. I walk on the grass, and here you are. You are always waiting for me.

Does anyone else see what I see?

You know I love you and can't wait to be near you. Christopher, I love to say your name.

I can say it a million times; for a mom, that is no shame.

It's so quiet. It's so peaceful. I don't stand for long. I can't help but kneel and look down.

Do you see me? I hope I don't frown.

Here you are, my son. Again, I visit you at the only place I know you can rest.

You stand out from all the rest.

I clean the dirt from your tombstone. I lovingly and achingly look at your name. I say your name because you can't.

I cry endlessly, can't help but mercifully chant.

I see your birth date engraved on the stone. I don't want to see the date when your life on this earth ended. It was the worst day of my life and for those who love you.

That tragic phone call—your motorcycle and that horrible car—it can't be true …

I had said I wished you could stay young forever.

Can I take those words back? Twenty-five years old is now your forever?

Will a miracle happen today, right now? Will I see a vision, a butterfly, perhaps a special bird?

Will there be a familiar voice heard?

Will my visit bring the touch of an angel wing? I so desperately need a present from you now.

I will accept anything, anywhere, anyhow.

Oh, what a selfish visitor I am. I am so sorry. But I bring you love and memories; I am here for you.

Thank you, my son. I needed this visit so much. It felt so good to cry at a solitary place.

I feel I can be free to open my broken heart at this sacred space.

Are you still here? If not, where are you? I so want to follow you. I ache to be with you.

I am so weary and brokenhearted, so lonely and blue.

I wish I could stay here forever. This is not enough. But I have others who depend on me.

I have to end this visit eventually, at this place and time, till the next time I'm free.

I must adhere to my responsibilities. I know you understand. I know you want me to go and do whatever needs to be done.

But it breaks my heart to leave you, my son.

I don't want to say good-bye. But I promise to come back very soon. I will have new decorations to bring you. Holiday wishes to share with you. I am sorry so many tears are left behind.

Son, no matter where I'm at, you are always on my mind.

I'm afraid you'll be lonely when I walk away. It's too hard to leave. I don't ever know if I should look back. Maybe I might see you standing there. But if I don't, my heart will break even more.

I lie down on your site, don't care if I get grass or dirt on me. It's you I adore.

I get in the car and pull out of the cemetery. As I drive down the road, no one is the wiser that I visited my son today. My moments with him at his graveside are all I have. It means so much to me.

My visits are private; I need them to breathe. I need to be at his side—don't you see?

A parent's work is never done.

A visit to my son.

About the Author

Lesia Schofer is a native and resident of Philadelphia, Pennsylvania. She is proud of her Ukrainian descent and heritage. She has been a teacher-librarian for more than thirty years, primarily in inner-city schools. She thoroughly enjoys reading to children. She is an avid reader and loves all animals dearly. Being a mother of two sons is a gift she cherishes. Losing one of her sons, Sgt. Christopher Schofer, to a tragic motorcycle accident is the reason for this work. Truth and loyalty to loved ones is important to her, as well as keeping memories alive. She believes it is a special world when individuals share what is deep within their hearts and souls with others.

CPSIA information can be obtained at www.ICGtesting.com
Printed in the USA
BVOW05s0013070815

412055BV00003BA/3/P